Please Protect the Porcupine

Bobby Boyd

Martha

Malcolm

Angie

Iggie

Courtnay

Miss Prim

Einstein

Muscles Mahoney

The Barbara Hazen Book of Conservation

Please Protect the Porcupine

with characters drawn by MELL LAZARUS
Creator of the nationally syndicated comic strip,
Miss Peach

A *Holly* BOOK

THE WORLD PUBLISHING COMPANY

Cleveland and New York

Published by The World Publishing Company
2231 West 110th Street, Cleveland, Ohio 44102
Published simultaneously in Canada by
Nelson, Foster & Scott Ltd.
First Printing 1967
Library of Congress Catalog Card Number: 67-25395
Printed in the United States of America

To Brack

May you always cherish, conserve, and care

Contents

THE PORCUPINE AND OTHER MATTERS

Why Should We Protect the Porcupine?

"Why should we protect the porcupine, Martha? Can't he take care of himself? With those long, sharp quills, he looks pretty well protected to me."

"He is, Bobby Boyd, from most other animals. But protecting him means a lot of other things too. It means making sure the porcupine has clean air to breathe and clear, unpolluted water to drink. It means the right kind of home for him and enough food so he doesn't have to fight over it. It also means seeing that he isn't hunted or harassed by bullies like Muscles Mahoney."

"Gosh, Martha. One porcupine needs an awful lot of protection, doesn't he?"

"We all do, Bobby Boyd."

Conservation—
What Kind of Preserve Is That?

"Children, do any of you know what conservation is? Do you know, Bobby Boyd?"

"Is it a kind of jam with the pits still in it, Miss Prim?"

"No, Bobby. Martha, can you tell me what conservation is?"

"Someone who wears old-fashioned skirts and high-button shoes and talks about how much better everything was in the good old days?"

"No, Martha. Malcolm, maybe you can help us?"

"I think conservation has something to do with saving, Miss Prim—like making the box of marshmallows last two weeks instead of gobbling them all down in a sitting."

"You're closest, Malcolm. Conservation has a lot to do with saving."

"Einstein, I see your hand. Maybe you can tell the rest of us what conservation is."

"Certainly, Miss Prim. Conservation is the care, proper use, and protection of land, water, wildlife, and other natural resources—because if we don't take care of what we have, we won't have it long.

"In more practical words, Miss Prim, please protect the porcupine, don't pick the wildflowers . . . and you might as well turn off the overhead light because there's plenty of sun coming in through the window, and electricity is a natural resource too."

11

Different Ways of Looking at It

"I can't stop thinking about conservation, Martha, and how it means different things to different people.

"To a sheepherder conservation means having plenty of good grazing land for his flock.

"To a fisherman conservation means clear, clean streams well stocked with fish.

"To a farmer conservation means rich topsoil and planting and plowing to make the most of his land.

"To a lumberman conservation means forest-fire control and reseeding forests so there will always be new young trees.

"And to Herman the hamster it means a daily supply of sunflower seeds, love, and lettuce."

Natural Resources
Versus Made-Up Marshmallows

"Stop eating and listen, Malcolm. What I'm saying is important. The resources of a country are all its assets—its most valuable possessions.

"And natural resources are these assets in their original state, untouched and untampered with. In other words, Malcolm, a natural resource is something just the way it came or grew—before it is manufactured or made up into something else. It is the tree *before* it is cut down and mashed into pulp for paper. It is the wool on the sheep *before* it is sheared off and knit into a mitten. And it is the egg exactly as the hen laid it, before it is beaten to a froth with sugar and gelatin and made into a marshmallow."

13

Courtnay's Chart of Renewable Resources

Renewable resources may become scarce, but they never run out. More are always on the way.

New trees will grow to replace the ones that were cut down.

New Tulips will bloom next spring.

New baby chicks will hatch from the hen's eggs.

There will be more water in the rain barrel after a good, hard rain.

Curls grow out after a too-short haircut. (Thank Goodness!)

14

Angie's Chart of Nonrenewable Resources

NON-RENEWABLE RESOURCES ARE
GONE FOREVER ONCE THEY ARE
USED UP.

THERE WILL NEVER BE ANY MORE--EVER!

MOST FUELS AND MINERALS, LIKE
OIL, COAL, AND GOLD.

ANY EXTINCT BIRD--
THE DODO IS GONE FOREVER.

THE CENTURIES-OLD STALACTITES
IN CRABTREE CAVERN, WHICH
ONE SUMMER OF SOUVENIR-SNITCHING
DESTROYED.

IRREPLACEABLE ART OBJECTS SUCH AS
THE OTHER HALF OF COLONEL CRABTREE'S
MOUSTACHE.

People Need Preserving Too

"No, Iggie, I will not pick up your stuffed crocodile! It's the umpteenth time you've tossed it out of the crib, and my patience, while renewable, is getting pretty thin.

"Maybe someday Einstein will develop a mechanical baby sitter. But until then, Iggie, it is essential that I conserve at least a little of my strength for the baseball game this afternoon."

Overpopulated and Underfed

"It's too late to do anything about it now, Angie. There would have been plenty of cake if you hadn't asked ten extra kids at the last moment.

"Don't you know that overpopulation, or too many people in one place, is one of the greatest reasons for running out of everything—from chairs to pieces of cake?

"That's why planning ahead is such an important principle of conservation—and of party giving."

"Malcolm, you may be slow at math but you're great at solving practical problems like Angie's cake crisis."

"It's kind of you to say that, Martha. But it seemed only good sense to ask the kids who already had cake to give half of theirs to the kids who had none. Because when you don't have enough, it's all the more important to make the most of what you have—to portion and pass it out fair and square.

"And speaking of sharing Martha, I really appreciate your letting me join you on the footstool. Sitting in that wastebasket was awfully uncomfortable."

Congressman Crabtree on the Balance of Nature

"Children, it is an honor and a privilege to be here today speaking to you about conservation.

"As you know, my great-great-great-grandfather was Colonel Crabtree, who was the founder of this fair city. It was he who sparked the revolution against tyranny and injustice that led to our freedom.

"Today I am here to spark another revolution, against the tyranny of ugliness, loss, and pollution that is threatening to take over our lovely land.

"Nature, children and future voters, must be balanced. And when man unwisely goes too far in any one direction and disturbs the balance of nature . . .

19

. . . the results are decidedly upsetting . . .

. . . which should not discourage the dedicated
conservationist or cause him to give up. Rather,
it should spur him on to persevere, pick himself
up, and do what he can, as quickly as possible,
to restore balance."

20

CRABTREE CORNERS CONSERVATION CLUB

"It's a beautiful sign, Martha. And organizing a Crabtree Corners Conservation Club was a great idea.

"Isn't it wonderful the way everything has worked out? Congressman Crabtree will be our honorary advisor, Courtnay said we could turn her playhouse into a clubhouse, Herman the hamster will pose for the wildlife armband, and Miss Prim donated an old bulletin board. Now all we need is some BIG, Meaningful, Very Important Project like stopping soil erosion on the moon or protecting a herd of wild elephants . . ."

"Or maybe, Bobby Boyd, you should look just beyond your nose and see what needs being done and saved right here. Those field mice who made a nest in the file cabinet look awfully hungry to me!"

21

WATER, WATER—WHERE?

Who Needs It?

"Water is not only important, it is a matter of life and death. Even desert rats and cactus plants have to have some water to drink.

"A garden has to have water to grow things.

"Bobby Boyd has to have water, because using grapeade in a water pistol isn't sporting.

"Fish have to have water to swim in, and a boat wouldn't float without it.

"Miss Prim needs water to clean the blackboard, and Niagara Falls couldn't put on its show without water.

"Angie needs water too. For while she might do very well without soap, even she couldn't exist without water."

A Few Facts, Ma'am

"Martha made a few good points, Miss Prim, but she left out some important scientific facts and figures.

1. That 75 per cent of this earth is covered by water.

2. That 60 per cent of all sports—camping, swimming, fishing, boating, skiing, and ice skating, for instance—need water or you can't play.

3. That raindrops often strike the earth at more than 30 miles per hour.

4. And that our bodies are made up of 70 per cent water, in spite of the nasty remark you just made, Martha, that mine must be mostly printer's ink and back-issue encyclopedias."

Fish Tanks

"No, no, Bobby Boyd! Putting in little fences to separate the fish isn't what the man in the pet shop meant by having a balanced aquarium. He meant that there should be a proper balance of kinds of fish, of numbers of fish to the space in the tank, and of plants to fish, and also the right amounts of food and oxygen so the fish stay happy, healthy, and full of swim and vigor."

. . . and Fishermen

"That's a beautiful bass on the end of your line, Malcolm. He's over the legal size and you're allowed to catch three. Besides, in a well-stocked, balanced lake, just as in a good aquarium, there will always be plenty more fish.

"*Truly*, Malcolm, you can be a conservationist and a fisherman too. Keeping what you caught is fine, so pull him in. What *is* unsportsmanlike is fishing illegally or polluting the water so that lots of fish sicken and die.

"You're a good sport, Malcolm—and I hope Courtnay will be one too when she finds it's her turn to put the worm on the hook."

Why Can't We Swim Here This Year?

"Honest, Martha, my curls aren't the reason I won't go in swimming! I'm just as hot as you and Angie are and just as disappointed after walking all this way. I don't mind a little healthy mineral matter, but this year Wilderness Pond is full of algae and scummier than last Saturday's split-pea soup.

"And I don't think you should go in either, at least not beyond your big toe. It smells funny and Uncle Iredell says you can get pretty sick from all that ick."

Marshmallow-Grapeade Is Not a Suitable Water Substitute

"Not another case of marshmallow-grapeade, Malcolm! Pretty soon there won't be any place in the clubhouse to sit."

"I'm only trying to do my bit for the future, Courtnay. Einstein says it is estimated that by 1980 the fresh water in our country will be used up. By that time we will be drinking re-used water, which will be harder and harder to make drinkable because of all the detergents and gunk and stuff in it."

"Then, Malcolm, we had better do something about water pollution right now, before it's too late. Instead of stashing away soda pop, write letters, get your neighbors interested in water conservation, and get good and mad at people who have nice boats but bad habits like tossing their sandwich crusts on the water . . . Because the rest of us are sick and tired of marshmallow-grapeade right now. Imagine how we'll feel by 1980!"

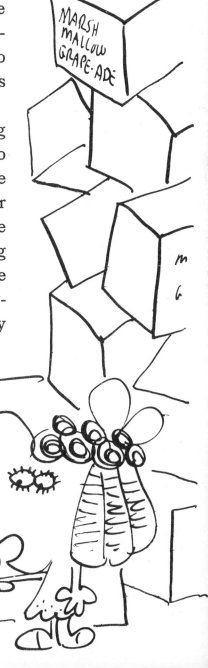

Social Science Quiz

Subject: Sewage

Q. Does your community have a sewage-disposal plant?

A. YES, INDEED, AND CHRYSANTHEMUMS, TOO!

Q. Is your local river water safe for drinking?

A. NOT IF YOU'RE LEANING OUT OF THE ROWBOAT AND BOBBY BOYD IS ABOUT TO HIT YOU IN THE TEETH WITH THE OARS. BUT IT IS PERFECTLY SAFE FOR DRINKING FROM THE TAP AFTER IT HAS BEEN FILTERED AND FIXED UP WITH CHEMICALS. (FILTERING KEEPS DRAGONFLIES FROM FALLING OUT OF THE FAUCET.) CHEMICALS, CAREFULLY ADDED, KEEP OUR WATER GERM-FREE AND AS CLEAN AS MISS PRIM'S KITCHEN.

Q. Is there a local dump?

A. THE BIG CITY ONE, OR ANGIE'S BACKYARD?

Q. How does your community treat its garbage?

A. WITH COURTESY AND COMPLETE INCINERATION

Every Drop Counts! And Every Drip Hurts

"You've got the right idea, Angie. While there's a water shortage, we each have to do what we can to save every drop.

"That means no lawn sprinkling except when Mayor Lindentree says so. And no water pistol fights. And don't ask for a glass of water if you aren't going to drink it. And if you aren't as thirsty as you thought, give what's left over to the daisies."

Save Water, but Please Wash

"Shut the faucets up tight so they don't drip and never fill the tub to the top. But, Angie, even Mayor Lindentree didn't mean not to wash at all—ever.

"Two inches will do the job nicely and then maybe Muscles will stop calling you the first human soil-conservation bank in Crabtree Corners."

What's a Water Cycle?

"Bet you don't know what a water cycle is, Bobby Boyd."

"What do you mean, Martha? My Uncle Arthur just bought a shiny black one. Vrrrroom! Zoooom! There he goes on it now."

"A water cycle, Bobby Boyd, is quite different from a Fundacycle. It is the never-ending cycle of water, falling and then evaporating, changing from one form to another. Water falls as rain or snow or sleet. Some of it soaks into the ground; some runs into rivers and streams. Eventually, from oceans, rivers, and plants, the water returns to the air as vapor. Soon it falls again . . ."

"Just like my Uncle Arthur! I'm sorry, Martha. Please go on."

"As I was saying, Bobby Boyd . . . Man has no control of the water cycle in the air. I mean, saying 'rain, rain, go away' doesn't really change the weather. But man can do a lot to control the water while it's on the ground. For instance, by keeping the soil covered with trees and grass he can cause more of it to soak in, which prevents floods in certain areas and water shortages in others. A big part of conservation is the study of ways to control the water cycle . . ."

"Which is a lot more than you can say of Uncle Arthur on his Fundacycle."

Help! Nature Needs Her Rain Barrel Too!

"What's that, Courtnay?"

"It's a double-duty padlock for the fence around my rain barrel, Einstein. If I don't protect it, bullies like Muscles Mahoney knock it over or fill it with mud. Rain water is great for rinsing your hair after a shampoo, you know."

"Know something else, Courtnay? Rain barrels are great for even more important things. Come with me and I'll show you one of nature's rain barrels."

"Einstein, this is Great Squishy Swamp. Bet there are snakes in it."

"And orchids, Courtnay, and gentians with fringes longer than your eyelashes, and many other rare plants and flowers—and beautiful water birds like that heron—and lots of animals. Great Squishy Swamp is a rare wildlife refuge and one of the few places around where no one but a blue jay ever screams at you.

"All swamps, marshes, and bogs are nature's rain barrels. And they are not only refuges and retreats for wildlife, but they also protect the towns around them from floods."

"Then we'd better protect Great Squishy Swamp from the people who want to drain it and build a shopping center. Einstein, I'm going to write Congressman Crabtree right now—and I'll donate my padlock to the Cause."

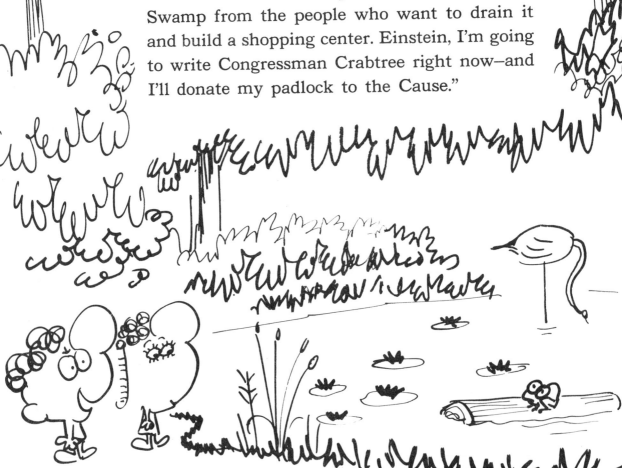

WHAT'S IN THE AIR?

There Was Bad Air in the Good Old Days Too

"Those were the good old days, Martha!"

"When, Courtnay?"

"Before automobiles and factories and atomic fallout, when the air smelled like April flowers instead of like last Tuesday's chemistry class."

"Air pollution is a problem, Courtnay. But it's not a new one. Air pollution began with the caveman's first wood fire. Air becomes contaminated when anything–soot, smoke, smells–is added to it.

"I said *anything*, Courtnay. 'Essence of Magnolia' counts too!"

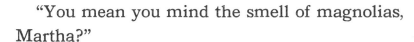

"You mean you mind the smell of magnolias, Martha?"

"Of course not, Courtnay, but a little goes a long way. That's what makes air pollution even worse now. There are so many people who put so many different kinds of things in the air. Einstein's experiments and Malcolm's leaf burnings and Angie's dust redistribution may all be worthy projects but they sure mess up the air.

"And if you don't mind my saying so, Courtnay, I'd enjoy my tea and cake a lot more if you'd use regular candles instead of the incense kind."

Trapped by a Lot of Hot Air

"Air pollution *is* mainly caused by people, Malcolm, but the problem is worse in different places. For instance, any city surrounded by hills is likely to have a lot worse air than a city out in the open. That's because the high hills trap the bad air and an air trap, or inversion, causes smog—which is a nasty mixture of smoke and chemical fumes. In an inversion, the dirty air is trapped by a layer of hot air above it.

"Get it, Malcolm? Now do you know what an inversion is?"

"Not exactly, but I sure know how one feels."

Protest Air Pollution!

"Angie, holding your breath till you turn purple is not the most constructive way to protest air pollution! *Do* something about the problem. Write Congressman Crabtree, organize a Clean Air Contest, have your father check his car—or get a horse, who burns fuel far more efficiently.

"But clean up your own atmosphere first. *You* may be able to exist in a dust bowl, but I'm going home to breathe."

What Do You Mean, Free Air?

"I can hardly believe it, Martha! Our Crab-tree Corners Conservation Club won the Clean Air Contest. The prize is an all-expenses-paid study trip to Soot City, and next week we'll be on our way. Great news, isn't it?"

"It is wonderful, Malcolm. But right now all I can think about is how much the new paint for the clubhouse is costing us. Dirty air certainly does a lot of damage. Besides ruining last year's paint job, it rots clothes and causes runny eyes. Did you realize that dirty air costs every man, woman, and child in this country over a hundred dollars a year in extra upkeep? And just think of how many marshmallows a year that could keep you in, Malcolm."

Seeing (?) Soot City

"Here we are, children, on the observation tower of the great Grill-Iron Building, which is the tallest building in our state's biggest city.

"On a clear day, according to the guidebook, you can see seven rivers, four states, and what the mayor is eating if there is an official picnic.

"Today, children, we will have to content ourselves with viewing the few bricks within easy reach and that—well, I *think* it's a pigeon.

"Now let's go inside to the gift shop and buy some post cards to see what we should have seen."

"And now, boys and girls, we are looking at the Amalgamated World-Wide Publishing Building, which was completed last January. It is a marvel of architecture and engineering . . . and I wonder why they are still working on it if it is finished."

"Oh, I know why, Miss Prim. The building was finished. But the chemicals and soot in the air ate holes through the rare metal columns and changed the colors of the murals—so now they are putting another sturdy, soot-proof front over the first front."

"But it's not nearly as beautiful as the one in the picture, Einstein. You mean the city has to protect its landmarks from its own air?"

"Yes, Miss Prim—just like Martha has to protect her fingerpaint posters from her own little brother, Iggie. Only soot is even worse."

"Aunt Abigail, I'm so glad I had a chance to see you on my afternoon off from sightseeing. It's fun to eat up on your little roof garden. Only I never heard of putting pepper on the outside of sandwiches before. . . .

"Oh, I see, Aunt Abigail. No, I don't mind a little soot. I'll try to talk less and eat quickly. . . .

"All finished. Now I can look at your dwarf daisies. . . .

"I see. I just didn't realize they were meant to be big, and I guess you *are* lucky to grow anything at all. I never realized bad air stunted plants. Golly creepers, if it does that to a daisy, what does it do to growing kids?"

Shape Up, Consolidated Central Public Power and Light!

"What's the matter with you, Einstein? I've never seen you look so angry."

"I *am* angry, Courtnay. Angry, and deeply disillusioned. Look out of the window. I just can't understand how they can do it."

"Who . . . do what, Einstein?"

"How Consolidated Central Public Power and Light, a company I have always looked up to and loved, can pour all that sulphur-polluted smoke into the air. Don't they know it's against the law? Don't they care about my sensitive sinuses and scientific feelings?"

"Golly creepers, Einstein, that *is* a dirty trick."

"You said it, Courtnay!"

Maybe Someday

Dear Mom and Dad,

Soot City is nice to visit but I'm glad I live in Crabtree Corners where I can smell a flower without getting my face dusty. Also, the people at home seem friendlier. Maybe that's because they can see better. The outside air is often so bad in Soot City that Aunt Abigail goes inside to get a breath of fresh air. I only hope Congressman Crabtree takes steps so that next time our class visits Soot City we can see it.

Meanwhile, please send my plastic underwater mask and diving suit to Aunt Abigail as a thank-you present to help keep out the soot when she serves tea on the roof garden. Love, Malcolm

SOIL IS A LOT MORE THAN DIRT

You Can Depend on It

"All of us depend on the soil, Bobby Boyd, even if you don't want it in your peanut-butter-and-grape-jelly sandwich. The peanuts in the peanut butter grew in the soil. So did the wheat that made the flour. And so did the grapevine.

"If it weren't for the soil, Bobby Boyd, plants wouldn't have places to put their roots. And they wouldn't be able to eat, because their food comes from the soil. Animals, too, depend on the soil for shelter and for the leaves and roots and berries they eat. Every living creature you can think of depends on the soil. And Angie depends on the soil more than any other living creature I can think of."

What's in It?

"For 'Show and Tell' today I brought a bag of genuine topsoil. Malcolm may giggle and call it 'ordinary dirt' but I would like to point out that good genuine topsoil takes centuries to become what it is, and it is a far from simple substance. In fact, genuine good dark rich topsoil is far less simple than Malcolm seems to be at times, being rich in minerals, the remains of plants, and countless organisms.

"Furthermore, given heat, light, water, and a seed in it, genuine topsoil is capable of producing a flower—and that's more than I can say for you, Malcolm."

Enemy of the Soil: Iggie Bulldozing

"Careless bulldozing, Iggie, is one of the most serious causes of soil erosion. And stripping the land of plants and trees not only makes a mess of the soil, but lots of houses without any shrubs or shade trees around them look pretty awful.

"But the worst problems in your play village will begin, Iggie, when the basements of all your toy houses fill with flood water and your whole shopping center washes into the wading pool."

A Good Garden

Should have loose soil.

Should have bits of decayed plants and animals.

Should be sunny.

Should have water, and good drainage, too.

Should be free of weeds.

May need extra food, like fertilizer.

Should have lots of lettuce, so Malcolm can make his special bacon, lettuce and marshmallow sandwiches.

A Bad Garden

IS A SAD GARDEN.

HAS SOIL AS DRY AND HARD AS CEMENT.

HAS ALL THE PLANTS POORLY SPACED
AND BUNCHED UP.

DOESN'T HAVE ROWS.

DOESN'T HAVE STAKES FOR THE LARGER PLANTS.

IS LIKE A DUST BOWL.

HAS LOTS OF LIMA BEANS.

NEVER SMILES BACK AT YOU WITH FLOWERS.

WILL TURN INTO A GOOD GARDEN IF YOU
GIVE IT FOOD, WATER AND LOVING CARE.

Suggestions for Improving Our School Grounds

"With just one exception, children, Principal Smothers and I are agreed that we will be able to incorporate all of your excellent suggestions into our Progress Plan."

A BIRD HOUSE IN EVERY TREE AND A FLOWER IN EVERY POT!

MORE LITTER BASKETS! IT'S A LOT EASIER TO BE TIDY WHEN THERE'S SOME PLACE TO TOSS THINGS.

PLANT A CLASS TREE -- SO MISS PRIM WILL HAVE SOME MEMENTO OF US, OTHER THAN HER COLLECTION OF CONFISCATED WHISTLES AND WATER PISTOLS.

A SHORTER SCHOOL WEEK. THAT WAY THERE WOULD BE LESS WEAR AND TEAR ON EVERYTHING!

YOU'VE GOT TO HAVE TREES

Our Leafy Green Friends

"Trees . . . just think of all they do for us, Martha.

"They shade us from the hot summer sun. They give us places for picnics. They provide places for birds to nest, and squirrels to hide their nuts. They are invaluable for tree houses, hide-and-seek, and places to hitch hammocks.

"Besides, Martha, trees are just nice to be near. They make lovely swishing sounds in the breeze, and they give us lacy, green leaf canopies to look through when we watch the clouds drift by."

"Right, Courtnay. And they also give us baseball bats and knotholes so we can watch what the kids next door are doing."

Big Oaks from Little Acorns

"Yes, Iggie. Little trees live in nurseries too. Little trees are called seedlings and they live in special seedling beds, just the way you have a special bed called a crib before you are old enough to be on your own in a big regular-sized bed.

"And little seedlings, Iggie, need just as much care and protection from wind, frost, drought, disease, bug bites, and excessive sunlight as you do.

"So put on your cap this instant, Iggie, or you won't grow up to be a healthy oak—I mean adult."

Our Class Plants

"Dig, Bobby Boyd. You can't plant our new class tree on top of the ground. The hole should be at least two feet wider than the roots so that they won't get cramped.

"Now I'll give the soil a shot of fertilizer . . . Manicure scissors, peat moss, mulch, water, supporting stakes, and step-by-step instruction book . . . Let's see, can you think of anything else I might need before it comes?"

"Maybe a nurse's cap, Courtnay."

"Our class tree. It is lovely, isn't it, Martha?"

"It certainly is, Bobby Boyd. Only I would like to make monster faces at the person who whittled *Daphne Loves Dimitri* on the tree trunk, which not only wounds the tree but defaces it for life. I mean, what self-respecting willow wants to live with a stupid saying like that the rest of its days?"

It's Enough To Make a Willow Weep

"Muscles Mahoney, you're a worse bully than I thought. What do you mean stripping the bark off that tree? Courtnay is far too good a conservationist to even read a note written on birch bark.

"How would you like it if someone pulled all the skin off you while your hands were up? If you have to pick on someone, pick on another big bully like you, who can at least hit back."

Tale of a Tree

"No, Courtnay, the redwood doesn't talk. That wasn't what the park director meant when he said it told a story. What he meant was that you can see what happened to the tree by looking at its stump.

"You can tell how old it was by the number of growth rings. You can also tell that it lived through several forest fires, and figure out the exact dates, depending on the location of the scars. And a careful look at the roots tells us about the floods the tree lived through.

"This tree, Courtnay, was 1,200 years old, and lived through four fires, two floods, and twelve bad cases of bark beetles."

"Amazing, Einstein, and a lot more accurate than my diary."

Select—Don't Just Hack

"The careful cutting of trees does not disturb a forest, Martha. Selective cutting and thinning make the new trees grow stronger and faster, just the way Courtnay says her curls grow better and faster after a haircut.

"Good lumbermen know this, Martha. It's the indiscriminate hacking away or cutting down too many trees at one time or in one place that causes floods, soil erosion, and loss of animal homes. Know-how and care make all the difference between a blighted, skinny set of bent-over trees and a full-treed beautiful forest."

"Okay. Okay, Bobby Boyd. I get the point. I'll never cut my own hair again—especially with poultry shears."

The Woods That Was

"Grandpa's woods *was* beautiful before the fire, Martha. All those trees that had been growing those hundreds of years—burnt away and gone because one camper was careless. The soil is scorched too, and there won't be any flowers or ferns this year.

"And all those poor homeless animals! Grandma only had room to take in ten deer, five field mice, four rabbits, three snakes, and one skunk with a slightly singed tail.

"It makes even me mad, Martha. It would have taken that camper just a couple of minutes to put out the fire completely. Now it will take a couple of lifetimes to see another woods where this one was."

IN THE YARD WHERE YOU LIVE

Carelessness

"Look at the mess you've made of your sand-box, Iggie. No wonder you don't want to play in it anymore.

"Even at your age, you should start taking a *constructive* interest in your surroundings. That's one of the goals of conservation. Because when you care about something, you're a lot more likely to take care of it.

"So, let's put fresh water in the wading pool, plow under the cookie crumbs, and clean up. It'll never be a rose garden, Iggie, but a couple of cactuses might survive."

. . . and Other Pitfalls

"Courtnay, someone should have told you that protecting the tender young grass shoots didn't mean covering them with Mother's new fur coat! Protecting a lawn means planting the grass seed, then keeping any other plants or weeds out. It means fertilizing the soil, watering the ground, and protecting the tender young shoots from bad bugs and bike wheels.

"Another thing, Courtnay. The too-close cropping of any lawn isn't a kindness. The good rich topsoil is much more likely to wash away, and then where will your grass blades be?

"So take back Mother's manicure scissors. Smile nicely at Muscles, and maybe he'll mow the lawn for you."

Flowers for Fun and All

"Mum's the word, pass it on."

"Martha, what on earth did Courtnay mean by that? Wasn't Mother's Day a while back? I'll bet this is another one of her silly secrets."

"Haven't you heard, Bobby Boyd? Courtnay and Angie are having a flower-garden contest. And Courtnay is excited because she has just found out there is a new kind of chrysanthemum that is highly disease- and insect-resistant —it drinks less water and doesn't like bugs."

"It *is* amazing what research is achieving in most fields, Martha."

"In flower gardens, too, Bobby Boyd."

The Soil Is Nature's Bank

"Try thinking of it this way, Angie. The soil is Nature's Bank. And the more you put into it, the more you get out of it. In other words, the richer the soil is in minerals and organic matter, the more flowers you will get out of it. And I doubt if even a self-respecting thistle will grow in three weeks' worth of house dust, laundry lint, and tracked-in mud."

Einstein's Scientific Analysis of One Square Foot of Topsoil in Courtnay's Garden

18 minerals (including one brass earring)

2 dead rhododendron roots

7 decaying leaves (3 with stems)

5 grubs

3 worms

4 and 1/17th ounces of water

¾ cup air

⅝ of a torn-up report card

½ garter snake

"Ugh, Einstein. Half a garter snake sounds awful. How did that happen?"

"Easily, Courtnay. He was halfway out of the test area when I measured him."

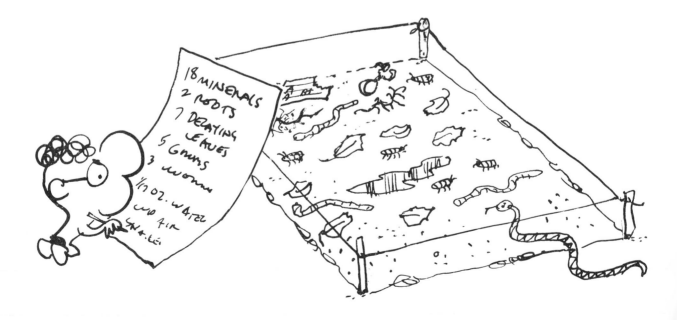

The Final Results: Angie's Flower Garden

"I got a fistful of dandelion seeds and blew them around—and they aren't weeds like Courtnay says because weeds are plants that aren't wanted and I *wanted* sunny yellow dandelions! I poked some other seeds in the ground, but I don't remember what kind.

"I guess I should have planted the tall flowers in back and chosen flowers whose colors go together.

"Maybe I should have dug rows too.

"Some of the blame goes to Muscles. First he dammed up the brook and caused a drought. Then he got a lot of old snowballs out of the freezer, put them in the brook, and caused a flood. . . .

"But mostly the fault is mine. I'm sorry, flowers. Next time I'll plan before I plant."

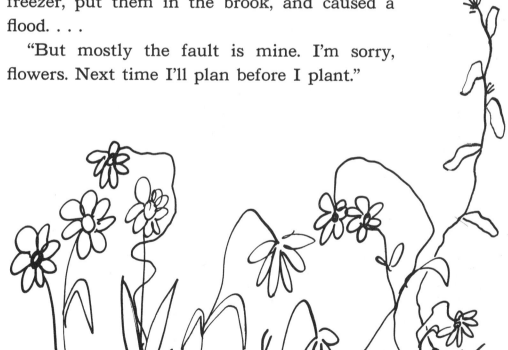

Courtnay's Garden

"First, I talked to the florist about what kinds of flowers would grow best in this climate and soil.

"Then I made a detailed plan of just what I wanted where.

"I fertilized the soil—plants need vitamins just as much as we do—and carefully prepared it. Then I planted the seeds several inches from each other in straight rows.

"Afterwards, I spent a lot of time weeding, watering, and cultivating my flower garden.

"You can see the results . . . and I'll also have flowers in the summer and fall because I planned it that way.

"And, Angie, here is a big bouquet for you!"

OUR FURRY FRIENDS

SOME ANIMALS GIVE FOOD. THE COW GIVES MILK, THE CHICKEN LAYS EGGS, AND THE CLAM GIVES CLAM CHOWDER.

SOME ANIMALS GIVE CLOTHING. WOOL COMES FROM SHEEP, SILK FROM THE SILKWORM, AND THE BRISTLES ON MY TOOTHBRUSH COME FROM A BIG BOAR.

ANIMALS DO OTHER USEFUL THINGS. HOMING PIGEONS CARRY SECRET MESSAGES, HORSES CARRY PEOPLE, AND ELEPHANTS CARRY TRUNKS.

WHICH IS WHY WE SHOULD TAKE CARE OF ALL OUR ANIMALS, BECAUSE THEY CAN DO A LOT OF THINGS BETTER THAN MAN CAN. I MEAN, BOBBY BOYD CAN'T LAY EGGS AND COURTNAY SURE CAN'T CARRY SECRETS.

Save Our Vanishing Wildlife

"Over a period of years, we who have studied conservation have learned to appreciate more and more the wonder and wisdom of nature's plan for the survival of her creatures. But there are times, my friends, when nature's design is changed by civilization—by the drainage of swamps and by the spread of cities and especially by pressures caused by overcrowding . . . And when this happens, we must all help nature preserve her vanishing creatures. . . ."

"Quick, Bobby Boyd. Help me catch Iggie before Congressman Crabtree compares him to the passenger pigeon or the dodo bird."

Not Every Hunter Is a Mean, Nasty Man

"Don't be ridiculous, Malcolm. Just because you found a buffalo robe in the attic doesn't mean you should take down your great-great-great-grandfather's portrait.

"Not every hunter is a mean, nasty man. And hunting is not necessarily against good conservation. For all you know this buffalo might have been charging the brave pioneer band, and single-handed your great-great-great-grandfather felled him with his bow and arrow. Even worse, perhaps the brave pioneer band was on the verge of starvation. And you've got to agree that twenty hungry pioneers meant more to the Wild West than one berserk buffalo."

Matilda the Mouser Is a Good Cat

"She isn't a bad cat, Courtnay, just because she caught a mouse. If it weren't for a few good mousers like Matilda, Crabtree Corners might be overrun by mice.

"Besides, the mice that are the fastest-footed get away. Matilda catches the ones that are slow or sick or wouldn't live long anyway. And her way is a lot more selective and kinder than a mousetrap. Nature controls the mouse population by animal agents such as Matilda. And she deserves a pat on the back and an extra cup of cream instead of a scolding."

There Are Several Ways to Shoot

"*You*, Malcolm, shot four wild ducks, two deer, and a baby rabbit at Grandpa's farm—and you want to show them to me?"

"Oh yes, Bobby Boyd. I've never done anything that was so much fun."

"Malcolm, this doesn't sound like you! Besides, hunting legally and with a license is one thing. But it's both unlawful and unsporting to bag any baby animal. Conservation doesn't mean no shooting. In some cases, hunting is even kinder than having animals starve because there isn't enough food for all of them. . . . But how could you shoot a baby rabbit?"

"Easy, Bobby Boyd. I did it with my new birthday camera. Besides, watching wildlife and photographing it is just as much of a sport as chasing it with a gun . . . you didn't really think I could . . ."

"Well, I'd rather not say anything except that he's a nice-looking baby rabbit and you take an awfully good picture."

Who's Game?

"Honestly, Bobby Boyd, I did not mean to insult Herman when I said he wasn't game. I know Herman is a good sport, but he is hardly a wild animal that is hunted for sport."

"That doesn't mean he isn't important, Malcolm. Animals can be valuable for lots of reasons —for fur, for food—or just for fun. And Herman is the funniest animal I know."

Who's Friendly?

"He's a nice doggie, Iggie. But don't pat him —not until his owner comes out of the store and we can ask if it's all right.

"Most dogs are as good natured as Malcolm, but once in a while you might meet one who's not used to one-and-a-half-year-olds or is in a bad mood because he got chased by the cat. And it's just as important to conserve kid brothers as any other kind of wild creature."

Don't Be Mean—or Silly

"Cruelty to animals, Malcolm, is doing something mean, like tying tin cans to a dog's tail or painting a pet turtle's back or throwing rocks at a squirrel.

"It is the irresponsible destruction of wildlife that the good conservationist is against. Some thinning down of the animal and bug population is necessary and a good thing. Otherwise the world might suddenly be overrun by jackrabbits or ground hogs.

"So you see, Malcolm, it's silly to refuse to leave your porch because you might step on another ant. Because to them you're a natural disaster, not an act of cruelty."

Think Before You Feed

"Cheer up, Iggie, the third little pig will be back at the Children's Zoo next week, and I promise you we'll come again.

"The park attendant said the third pig was coming around nicely. Three pennies, a paper-wad, and ice cream with the stick in it would make anyone feel funny. I don't imagine any person here would deliberately poison an animal, but every day some animal gets sick because a person thoughtlessly fed him something that was bad for him. That's why I got several of the crackers that are made especially for the animals—I said, the *animals*, Iggie."

The Animals Are for Real

"Absolutely not, Iggie! So stop kicking up your heels and crying.

"Sure the baby chicks are fluffy and cute, but I am not going to buy one for you. You don't have the right kind of place to keep it. You might pat it too hard and hurt it. And what would you do when it started missing its mother or you got tired of it?

"A live animal is not a toy, Iggie. When you are considerably older and wiser and can treat it properly, you can have some kind of pet. Meanwhile, enjoy looking at the live ones, but stick to the stuffed kind at home."

IT'S FOR THE BIRDS

The Bald Eagle:
A Good Example of a Rare Bird

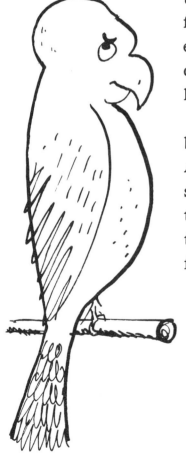

"This is a picture of a bald eagle. Note his curved beak and sharp talons and brave look. That is because he is a very important bird. In fact, he is our national emblem, the living symbol of the might and power of the United States.

"But even a brave bald eagle has problems. And his problem is that he is fast disappearing. For the bald eagle lives mostly on fish and likes to build his nest near the water. People, too, like fish and waterfront lots. And too many bald eagles have become discouraged after swooping down to the shore, to find a summer cottage in last year's nesting site.

"So there aren't many bald eagles left. The bald eagle is indeed becoming a rare bird. The Audubon Society has built sanctuaries to help save him. And I have saved my pennies to send to the Audubon Society, along with Uncle Arthur's old hairpiece, which would make a perfect nesting place."

Nobody Wants a Worrybird

"Malcolm, you have got to stop brooding about it! Certainly you have a right to be concerned about the decreasing numbers of waterfowl and bald eagles. Nobody wants them to become extinct.

"And *everybody* is worried about the whooping crane. With only 43 left at last count, conservationists are redoubling their efforts to protect the big bird and provide him with safe, suitable breeding grounds. You aren't the only one who wants to get the whooping crane on the nest and off the 'Rare and Endangered' list.

"But remember the Conservation Club Motto: *'Do, Don't Stew.'* You, Malcolm, can't personally make the Canadian whooping crane lay more eggs, but you can get up and get some birdseed out on the ground for the feathered friends in your own yard who haven't had a decent dinner since the snowstorm."

Feed That Seed

"One thing you can say about Malcolm, Martha, is that when he finally decides to do something, he does it right. His is by far the most efficient and interesting bird feeder in Crabtree Corners."

"You can say that again, Bobby Boyd. It's the only one I've ever seen with fountains for drinking water, turrets that hold ten different kinds of seed, and a drawbridge that automatically pulls up in case of a cat."

I Do Not Eat Like a Bird!

"Don't cry, Courtnay. Malcolm didn't *mean* to insult you when he said you 'ate like a bird.'

"Malcolm was simply misinformed. Little did he know the true facts: that almost no other animal eats as fast or with such great gusto–that a pair of flickers can toss off 5,000 ants at one sitting, and that a cedar waxwing feels just great after gulping down 100 cankerworms. And a martin can do a much better job of mosquito control than a man. For instance, one bird can gobble and get rid of 2,000 mosquitoes in one day, –which is pretty hard on the bugs but awfully good for the balance of nature–and for us."

Feathered Friends Forever

"All I've done, Martha, is give the birds food and water and a place to live.

"That's nothing compared to what they've done for me. Every morning they wake me up with a song, which is a lot better way than with an alarm clock. And at breakfast they put on a better show than the color TV. And I'm enjoying them even more, now that I have a bird-identification book that tells their names and all about them.

"Birds are just like best friends. The more you get to know them the better you like them."

"Which obviously works both ways, Malcolm."

Don't Badger the Birds!

"I don't care if you didn't actually pull the feather out of the peacock's tail, Iggie. You chased it till he dropped it out of sheer exhaustion, and that's a crime against conservation. Teasing an animal is almost as bad as deliberate meanness, like throwing rocks or robbing a robin's nest.

"You can't give it back, Iggie, but you can apologize and be nicer next time we come to the Children's Zoo."

NOT ALL BUGS ARE PESTS

Even an Ugly Bug
May Be Somebody's Friend

"Don't you think it is a bit rash, Courtnay, to say that something ought to be done about all the beetles just because this one pinched you?

"A few *are* big pests, but a lot of beetles, like the ladybug and the lightning bug, are our friends. Besides, I think you'll have to forgive this particular beetle when you realize that the stag beetle, or pinching bug, is attracted by *anything* that glows."

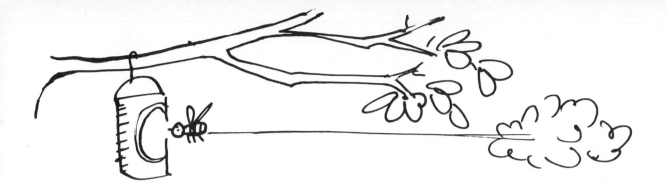

Getting the Bad Bugs Without Hurting the Good Guys

"The bugs **that are** pests can be controlled in a number of ways. **And** one method, Courtnay, is biological control. **That** means knowing the life cycle and habits of one 'wanted' bad bug so well that you do something to kill him off without hurting any of the good, beneficial bugs in the same area.

"For instance, Courtnay, a small special kind of black light is invisible to man but lures many kinds of flying nuisances to their doom. It's a lot less expensive than pesticides. And safer, too. Besides it's a scientific fact that, with a few exceptions like the firefly, most bad bugs do their dirty work at night. Good bugs fly during the daytime.

"Nature has her own way of controlling pests. One bird does better than a pound of pesticide. See that woodpecker working away? He won't hurt the tree but he will keep the bark beetle population down. And bark beetles have destroyed more trees than forest fires ever did."

"Then the woodpecker is really doing your yard a big favor, isn't he, Einstein?"

"He certainly is, Courtnay. Those beetles are so sneaky they hide under the bark, where even the tree surgeon has trouble finding them. I mean, sometimes it takes a natural enemy, rather than a medical man, to cure the pest problem."

You Can Get Sick of It

"I didn't mean to imply that all pesticides were bad, Courtnay. There are some good, effective ones that control pests but don't hurt the friendly bugs or endanger the people who feast on the harvest. What's more, after they work, these insecticides are made harmless by elements in nature. They don't end up polluting the water supply or poisoning the soil, which in turn poisons the meadow grass, the cow that grazes on it, and, eventually, us. . . . The wrong kind of pesticides or the improper use of a particular pesticide, however, often results in a situation where, eventually, the bad bugs come on even stronger. . . ."

"Please, Einstein. No more talk today. But I do know what you mean. Because the same medicine that cured my infected little toenail last year isn't doing a thing for it this year. I guess you can become immune to anything."

DEAR CONGRESSMAN CRABTREE :
    I WOULD LIKE TO KNOW
HOW YOU STAND ON MOSQUITOES.

    PLEASE LET ME KNOW
ANY SPECIFIC MEASURES YOU
HAVE TAKEN BECAUSE I WOULD
LIKE TO BE AS WELL-INFORMED
AS POSSIBLE.
                    SINCERELY,
                    BOBBY BOYD

Dear Bobby Boyd:

It is hard to take a firm stand on mosquitoes, as anyone knows who has tried.

However and furthermore I want you to know that state-wide I am doing all I can to push proper pest control and practice conservation, and that my own pond upstate is perfectly clean.

As to your question on whether I have taken specific measures, my answer is that it is well-nigh impossible to measure the tiny critters accurately.

I thank you, son, for your interest and enthusiasm and am sending you a "Be Kind to Critters Button" and a copy of my latest filibuster entitled "Caterpillars at the Crossroads of Our Community."

Cordially,

Your Congressman,

F. Myron Crabtree

F. Myron Crabtree

THE GREAT OUTDOORS—LET'S
KEEP IT THAT WAY

A Vista Should Be a View You Want to See

"I'm not arguing that Crabtree Corners shouldn't have a vista, Einstein. Every town worth its park commissioner should have several parking and recreation areas out in the surrounding hills—so people can picnic and look down and enjoy the view.

"What the rest of us in the Conservation Club object to is where you suggest putting it. Combustion may be fascinating to you, Einstein, but the rest of us would much rather gaze down on Wilderness Pond than the city incinerator."

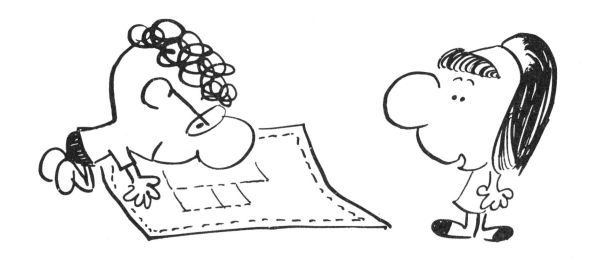

Let's Not Do the Urban Sprawl

"No, Muscles. The Urban Sprawl is not a new dance. It's a special problem progress has created. It's the growth of the city into the surrounding countryside, which crowds the land and makes it all the more important for conservationists to plan and set some areas aside for parks, playgrounds, and camp sites. Otherwise little kids like Iggie won't have any woods to go to when they get big enough to carry their own bedrolls."

Let's Keep It Wild

"Look at well-meaning Malcolm, trying to rub the moss off stones to give them a smoother, more polished appearance. Somehow I don't think he has quite the right idea about natural beauty—which means don't touch, just leave the rough-hewn loveliness the way it is."·

Let's Keep Going

"Einstein, in every camping trip or any kind of outing, there is a time to gather knowledge and a time to act; a time to contemplate and a time to *get moving*.

"So put down that slide rule and help me set these arrows and markers along Wilderness Trail. The next campers who come along will be a lot more grateful for knowing the names of the flowers and which way the pond is than they will be in knowing the exact algebraic ratio of Queen Anne's lace to buttercups per square yard of topsoil."

Angie, There Are Constructive Ways to Break Up Camp

"Stop it, Angie. Tearing the paper plates isn't what the park attendant meant by 'breaking up camp.'

"He meant to tidy up and take things down and leave the camp ground the way you would like to find it if you were the next camper—no tent-stake holes, or paper cups, or tin cans to trip on. And drown that campfire till you're double sure it's out. That's a lot more important than anything!"

Progressive Park Planning

"Gosh, Einstein, is that the plan you're going to submit to the new Park Commissioner?

"The sculptured play equipment is fascinating, and the rubber matting under the swings is a wonderful safety feature. It's bright and imaginative, from the rocket-shaped slide to the water fountain disguised as a computer.

"All that progressive stuff has a point—but Iggie might not understand unless you have a sandbox too. . . . And don't you think there should be some kind of entrance?"

Vest-Pocket Parks

"No, Bobby Boyd, a vest-pocket park is not a pocket in which to put Herman the hamster. It is a little oasis of beauty, often in the middle of pretty dreary city surroundings. It is a place to sit in the sun and enjoy a change of scene and contemplate something green and growing. It is a little corner of quiet in the middle of a lot of hustle and bustle."

"You mean you don't think hamsters have the same needs, Martha?"

National Parks Can Be All Kinds of Places

"That was an interesting and original approach, Malcolm, but I don't think you have it quite right. The Department of the Interior is not concerned with the contents of anyone's stomach. What the Department of the Interior does care deeply about is the contents of our country—its forests, waterways, and wilderness areas—and in saving these things in their original beauty and usefulness.

"Last year alone, the National Park Service, part of the Department of the Interior, opened over 2,000 new camping sites. So you see, a map of our national trailways would have been a lot more relevant to today's social science discussion than your diagram of the digestive tract."

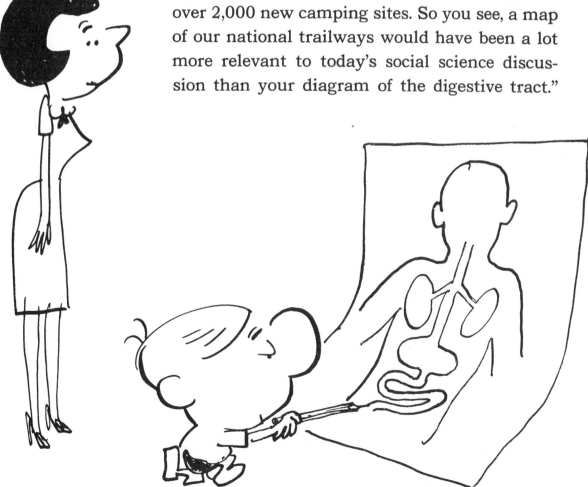

National Parks

"There are all kinds of parks, Courtnay. There are parks on historic sites, and parks where you can dig fossils or study Indian crafts. There are parks especially for fishing, skiing, swimming, boating, scientific study—anything you name probably has a park for it.

"There are different kinds of camping ·areas too. Some *are* rough and rugged wild places without even a foot path. But the one we're going to has trash cans, tent sites, running water, and even picnic tables. I still think you're silly, though, to load your bedroll with embossed paper napkins when leaves do just as well and are a lot more fun."

Public Beach Is a Dirty Shame

"What's Courtnay doing with that silver thing around her neck?"

"It's a sun reflector, Malcolm. She's trying to get a faster tan."

"But she went to Public Beach yesterday, didn't she?"

"Sort of, Malcolm. She said the traffic was so bad that they had the picnic in the middle lane instead of by the sand dunes. And when they finally got to the beach, it was so crowded they couldn't find the water. And when they did it was too dirty and full of gunk to swim in.

"So this morning Courtnay smashed her piggy bank, spent half of the money on a sun reflector, and sent the rest to the conservation people in the Capitol asking them to please do something before next swimming season."

Where Is the Wilderness That Was Here Last Year?

"I'm sorry, Courtnay. I didn't mean to be rude. But this was my favorite secluded spot and I didn't expect to find anyone here—especially girls giggling and playing Old Maid.

"I just don't know where to go any more to get away from the pressures of Little League and my paper route. There's a traffic jam of canoes on Lost Lake and you have to stand in line for pole space at my favorite undiscovered fishing hole. Hidden Canyon has more hot dog stands than ground hogs and I just saw a traffic sign on Wilderness Walk.

"And if somebody doesn't do something about it soon, there won't be any real rugged wilderness left, and the last frontier will be the lost frontier."

100

Operation Golden Eagle

"Just look at Malcolm with his black leather jacket with the golden eagle on it. Do you suppose he's joined up with my Uncle Arthur in some secret Fundacycle society?"

"Don't be silly, Bobby Boyd. Malcolm has joined something. But it is a wonderful and worthy cause called Operation Golden Eagle. It's a government program and its purpose is to make more Americans aware of the need to make more land and water available for parks and recreation purposes.

"Their motif, Bobby Boyd, is a golden eagle soaring into the sky...."

Golden Passport

"Boy, Martha, aren't we lucky that Malcolm's father has a Golden Passport. That means the rest of us won't have to pay anything to get in the national park. It not only admits the person who bought it but anyone else who comes in the car with him. That's generous of the Government, isn't it!

"Especially when you consider Malcolm's father has a super-deluxe giant size station wagon that seats three adults, six kids, several dogs, and even has a side pocket for visiting hamsters."

Fun on the Fungus Field Trip

"I'm surprised at you, Malcolm, saying that the Fungus Field Trip is the best Conservation Club outing ever because I brought along a box of marshmallows to roast afterwards. The true purpose of the trip is the scientific study of the fungi of the upper Crabtree Corners wilderness area."

"I am interested in fungi, Martha. I enjoy eating mushrooms and kicking puffballs. But learning is *always* easier when it's connected with fun—and, for me, marshmallows are more fun than anything!"

"Don't look worried, Miss Prim. This mushroom would be perfectly safe to eat if you felt like eating it. You can tell because of its cream color and prominent vertical ribs on the cap. It is not crumbled or convoluted like the cap on the false, or poisonous, variety.

"Learning the positive identification of plants is not only one of the interesting facets of a study of conservation, but it's been a wonderful way to stretch my allowance.

"So happy birthday, Miss Prim. And my feelings aren't at all hurt, because you still think it's safer not to eat it. Actually I'm far more flattered that you intend to stuff it and put it on your knickknack shelf."

104

Save Our Beach,
the Biggest Sandpile of All!

"Every bit counts, Iggie. The little patch of sand you are planting dune grass on may not look like much, but if everybody on Sunset Island plants a square foot, Dune Grass Day will be a success. And if it is a success, next year when we come here on vacation, the lovely sandy dunes will still be here, because dune grass holds the sand and keeps it from blowing, which will be nice in a lot of ways. Then maybe the peanut butter sandwiches won't be crunchy even when you buy the smooth kind."

Not All Progress Needs to Be Paved

"I am not against progress, Bobby Boyd. But I am against a paved bicycle path six lanes wide on Sunset Island. Who needs it! The lovely dirt path works fine and is a lot more fun. Besides, Sunset Island wouldn't be such a good place to go to get away from Crabtree Corners if it looked just like Crabtree Corners.

"Once in a while, Bobby Boyd, it's nice just to go slow, and look around, and sniff the summer breeze, and think about morning glories and sand castles."

OUR RESOURCES ARE LIMITED

A Paper Clip Can Be Precious

"No, Courtnay, our mineral resources are not unlimited! How easy and unthinkingly all of us take and consume, taking for granted that there is an endless supply.

"But that just isn't so. Our reserves are fast being used up. In fact, we are about to run out. . . . So I might as well tell you just how critical the situation is, Courtnay. If you take that last paper clip to pin back your hair, I won't have anything to hold the minutes of the meeting together."

Mine It Right!

"Proper mining is one thing, Muscles Mahoney. Improper mining scatters the topsoil, disturbs the wildlife, and leaves an ugly heap on one side and a gaping hole on the other.

"So if your hound dog keeps scarring my yard and strip mining the ground for bones in such a careless way, I'm going to have to report him to the Conservation Club."

Every Person and Power Plant Needs Go Power

"Man's progress depends on energy, Iggie. Man power, animal power, water power, electric power —and, in the future, atomic and solar energy.

"So spoon up your oatmeal, drink your milk, and renew your own resources of boy power."

Energy from Fire

"Fuels create energy too, Bobby Boyd. When coal—or oil or gas or wood—burns, its energy is changed to heat, which warms us."

"I know, Martha. I can feel it. But I wonder if we should have started burning the coal so soon. What if the fire dies before Malcolm comes with the marshmallows?"

"Don't be such a worrier, Bobby Boyd. We won't run out of coal as long as we are careful. Being good conservationists we must make our fire efficiently and use our resources wisely. Today's planning will help prepare us for tomorrow's world."

"And tonight's marshmallows, Martha."

Maybe Someday Atoms

"Einstein, atomic energy may, indeed, be the hope of the future. I *know* that Consolidated Central Public Power and Light has just built a modern atomic power plant upstate that doesn't have one single smokestack to dirty the air. I *realize,* furthermore, that atomic energy has successfully powered submarines, which means they don't have to keep going to the surface to refuel. Finally, I am *fully aware* that atomic energy has the advantage of being one resource we can never run out of.

"But I still say that for the moment we in the Crabtree Corners Conservation Club are going to have to content ourselves with light from ordinary electric light bulbs."

. . . or Maybe the Sun

"I just love to lie in the sun, Martha. But one thing I don't understand. If the strength of the sun's energy hitting a house roof is 100 times stronger than the energy carried by electric-power lines, why do I always feel sleepy when I take a sunbath?

"And if, as Einstein says, solar, or sun, energy may someday run our furnaces, refrigerators, and even factories, why does it slow me down instead of speeding me up?"

"I don't know, Courtnay. Some things are beyond third grade."

Boy Power: A Few Kinds of Energy
Can Be Increased

"Martha, your physical fitness program sure has changed Iggie. I can hardly believe the difference. His cheeks are rosy and his nose has stopped running. His arm muscles no longer feel like mashed potatoes, and he has more energy than a new electric train. He even acts better. This is the first time we have ever finished a Monopoly game without his whining, whimpering, and having at least one tantrum on the Boardwalk."

"No doubt about it, Bobby Boyd. Iggie's a lot nicer to live with now that he's shaped up and knows the difference between a popsicle and a pushup."

NATURE HAS A CERTAIN ORDER

Please Plan

"Left to herself nature keeps a certain order, which is more than anyone can say for you, Angie.

"Summer always follows spring, low tide always follows high tide, and day always follows night. Otherwise none of us, from school kids to early birds, would know what to do.

"So if nature can plan years at a time, for all the countries in all the continents, the least you can do is plan one day at a time. That way you just might get to school on time, and even have time for breakfast."

Don't Be Wasteful!

"You are right, Malcolm. Grownups should know better. They should care about conservation just as much as kids. But you can't honestly be *too* angry at great Aunt Abigail because she left the water running when lightning struck the roof and the cat knocked over the china cabinet.

"Sometimes a gentle reminder is in order . . . but a *gentle* reminder, Malcolm. A few words to the wise should be sufficient."

Don't Mess It Up

"Of all the creatures in the world, man is the only animal that wilfully destroys his own environment.

"A beaver wouldn't dream of smashing his dam in a fit of temper, and no self-respecting woodpecker would drill down the tree that feeds him.

"Man alone goes around making something and then making a mess of it. You did it, Iggie, and you're going to have to clean it up—or live with it!"

Litter Bugs Are the Biggest Pests

"There's nothing like a walk in the country, away from the sound of the car horn and the smell of the smog. Wonderful isn't it, Courtnay? The air is so clean and fresh and clear—even the squirrels seem brighter-eyed and bushier-tailed. Oh, let's skip and scatter the leaves as we go."

"Leaves, yes, but please don't drop your banana peels, Martha. Leave the countryside the way you like to find it. Don't you know litterbugs are the worst recurring pests conservationists have to fight!"

But Litterbags Are Great

"This is *not* some new-fangled kind of container for my hair curlers, Martha. It is a litterbag.

"Everyone should have one—for beach parties and picnics, car trips and boat rides. Because keeping their trash contained is the responsibility of everybody who uses the out-of-doors for fun.

"As Congressman Crabtree says, 'You *can* take it with you!'—right in your own litterbag."

Use Your Head, Time Is Valuable Too

"I believe in the practice of conservation just as much as you do, Angie, but common sense has a place in it too.

"Watering the class philodendron with your left-over drinking water makes sense if there is a shortage. And leaving string on the window ledge to help the birds build their nests is considerate. And of course your drive to collect and reuse paperclips saves both money and metal.

"I know your intentions were good, Angie, but don't you honestly think writing your entire composition on the back of a used postage stamp was more a waste of time than a conservation of paper?"

Preserve Historic Landmarks
and Meaningful Footprints
in the Sands of Time

"You're right, Bobby Boyd. History *is* a record of important past events, a meaningful account of earlier times, people, and even animals.

"And a historic landmark is an especially treasured relic of the past, whether it is an Indian relic or the Liberty Bell, an early invention or a dinosaur track. These are landmarks to be preserved and conserved.

"But don't you think that casting Herman's tracks in cement is going a bit far, Bobby Boyd? Do you think posterity will really care?"

Preserve What You've Done

"Early man knew a lot more about conservation than you do, Iggie. He wanted to save what he made.

"In Mesa Verde, Colorado, you can still see the well-preserved remains of an entire city built under the protective overhang of a cliff. And the cliff dwellers who built the city centuries ago had only the most primitive tools and their bare hands.

"You, Iggie, have ten kinds of plastic tools, silly putty, and little blocks that snap together.

"The architectural creation of the cliff dwellers will live forever. Can't you at least keep your block house up till suppertime?"

Conservation Means Making the Most of It

"Conservation means not wasting what you have, Courtnay, whether it's water or a talent for making things look nice.

"Just because you are terrified of wiggly things and would really rather sleep in your own bed than on the ground and the vote was unanimous against your suggestion for a blue cement sidewalk from the top of Lookout Hill to the pond, doesn't mean we don't want you in the Conservation Club. Personally I have thought it over at great length and decided that your suggestion for a scenic footpath around the poison ivy should definitely be considered and would be a fine contribution to Crabtree Corners."

NATURE HAS LAWS—JUST LIKE MISS PRIM AND MOTHER

"Thanks for asking me to football practice, Bobby Boyd. It's helping me a lot with my term paper on *Nature's Laws of Life*."

"Huh, Courtnay? How?"

"The law of adaptation, Bobby Boyd, is aptly demonstrated by the fact that the players play the game quite differently on a muddy field from the way they play on a dry one.

"And the same law of protection, of safety in numbers, that applies to animals in a group applies to those boys in a huddle. For example, it is a lot easier to tackle one lone player or sheep that has strayed than take on the whole herd, I mean team.

"*Control,* Bobby Boyd, is another one of nature's laws. Too many boll weevils or bears running unchecked in a garden is just as out of order as too many players on the football field.

"And the natural law of *multiplication* is clearly shown by the boys on the bench. When one player leaves the game, another is ready to take his place. Otherwise, fullbacks might become as extinct as the dodo bird.

"Finally, as in nature's rule book, there are penalties for unnecessary roughness and the whole team is penalized when one person is off balance."

And We've All Got To Live Together

"Plants and animals live together, Iggie. They depend on each other. The bee depends on the clover for nectar to make his honey, and the clover depends on the bee to carry pollen around so there can be more clover.

"No living thing, no plant or animal is totally independent. And if the clover and the honeybee can get along to the benefit of both, why can't we?

"Don't you think one and a half is a little young to run away? And I can tell you're hungry by the way you're chewing on your stuffed crocodile. Come on back, Iggie, I'll even put some of that delicious honey on your pabulum. You can depend on the bee—and on me."

Nature Puts on an Even Better Show Than the Seniors

"You know, Martha, nature puts on an even greater show than the one the seniors did. Just look at all the action that's taking place in this one spot in the woods. A mother robin is feeding her baby birds, a shy raccoon is looking at us from that hollow log, a rabbit is sitting in a

clump of violets, and there are ten kinds of ferns and twenty kinds of flowers in the scenery.

"Also the curtain *never* comes down, even though the scene is constantly changing, hour to hour, season to season, and place to place."

"It's the greatest show on earth, Courtnay, and it's up to us kids to keep it that way."

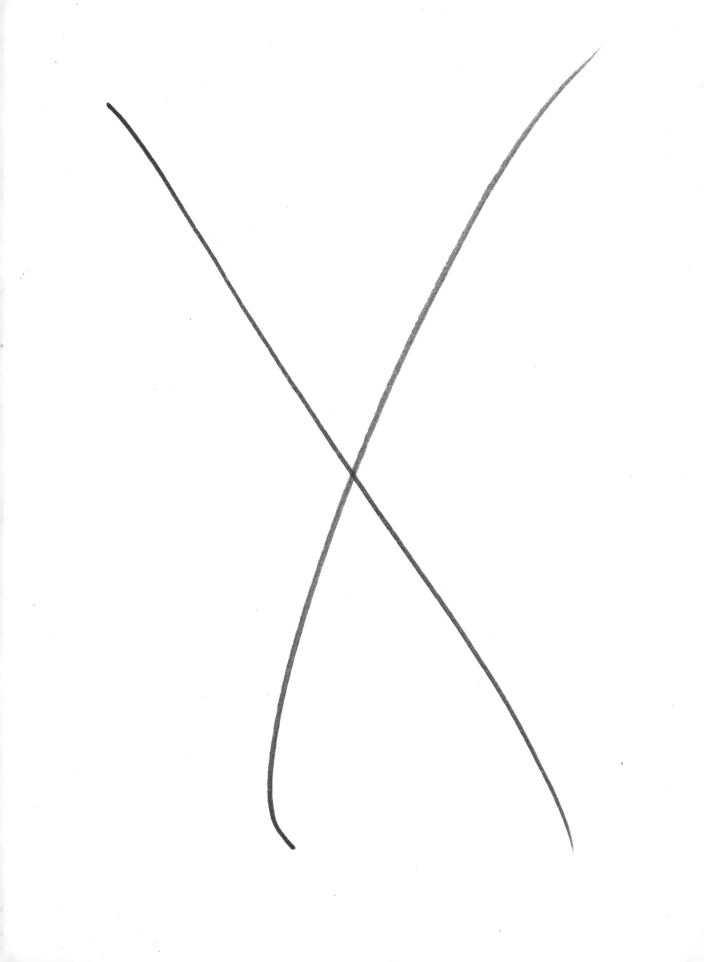